WOMEN'S FASHION AND POLITICS.

How they have influenced each other in the contemporary age.

TABLE OD CONTENTS

INTRODUCTION

With the turbulence of world politics at the present time it is impossible to miss media stories and articles published about the clothing of women in politics. It is from here that this EPQ idea started to take shape. The aim of this project is to find out the extent of the influence that politics and fashion have on each other. To do this, topics such as different periods of history (all within the contemporary age from approximately 1945 to the present day), the public opinion about dress and the extent of the political influence on it, and the role of the media will be covered. To create the content for this project extensive primary and secondary research was carried out. A questionnaire was created which was sent to women involved in both local and national politics in an effort to get their opinions and included their responses in this essay. For the secondary research extensive reading was carried out and notes made on the sources found, which can all be seen in the reading log and bibliography. Books, academic journals, magazine and newspaper articles and documentaries were used, only from credible sources.

This research is so important because of the unpredictable political times that we are living in today. The US election in November shot the Trump and Clinton families further into the spotlight, showing them in many garments through the media worldwide, so much so that Hillary Clinton's signature style of trouser suits has been made famous. The same can be said of the 2016 British general election, although arguably on a less global scale, with more focus on female politicians such as Theresa May and Nicola Sturgeon. Important political events such as the controversial 'Brexit', with the added help of social media, have caused a national surge of politics coming up in everyday conversation, possibly unlike any other time. This has triggered many more political meetings and events to which different outfits must be worn giving the media new opportunities to comment on the clothing of all female politician, including anything from Theresa May's leopard print kitten heels to Nicola Sturgeon's 'radical' style transformation (Bazaar, 2017 – reading log no. 5). The same level of importance should also be given to the influence of fashion houses. Big haute couture houses are increasingly political with the designs they put out on the runways, such as the statement political T-shirts seen at 2016 fashion weeks worldwide, an example being Dior's 'We should all be feminists' T-shirt, debuted in their Spring Summer 17 collection (Bryant, 2016 – reading log no. 8).

The research in this project is only focused on women and the political world (i.e. no focus on the business world or other areas) to enable the research to be more specific and to be able to research more deeply into a more niche topic.

Through the research and evidence set out in this project, the intention is to highlight the influences that politics and fashion have on each other, answering the title question through three sub topic questions to allow for a clear conclusion.

LITERATURE REVIEW

Both fashion and politics are concepts that have been around for thousands of years. The word 'politics' derives from the Greek word 'politikos', defined as 'of, for, or relating to citizens'. The word 'fashion' is derived from the Latin verb 'facere' meaning to make or do; i.e. to make or change one's appearance (for the better) through the use of clothes. Despite this, women did not enter the British parliament until 1918 when Countess Constance Markievicz became the first woman to be elected to the House of Commons, seventy years after women's suffrage began. Before this, in the 19th century, women had absolutely no place in national politics (Parliament, 2017 – reading log no. 36). It has not been until recent times that the connection between politics and fashion has been made. To add to this, women have been interested in keeping up their appearances for thousands of years. We can date early women's fashion back to the Roman period (27BC – AD180), when social class was a big factor in what women wore. Wealthy women would wear expensive silks, bright colours, and gold jewellery, while working class, poorer women would wear basic linen tunics. Today, factors such as the internet, the invention and high use of social media, as well as mass media, and the range of topics they cover, have all contributed highly to the link made between politics and fashion. This in turn has allowed a greater public interest in the link to flourish.

A fundamental link between politics and fashion is that fashion influences the politician in how they feel and how they are portrayed in the media, and, therefore, how they come across to the public. Fashion influences politics as current political events (such as the controversial topic of feminism) allow designers to express their political opinion through the design of their clothes, which are predominantly shown to the public through their runway shows. A recent example of this was a T-shirt with the slogan 'We should all be feminists' debuted at the Dior Spring Summer 17 runway show. (Bryant, 2016 – reading log no. 8). This design was inspired by Chimamanda Ngozi Adichie's book length essay titled 'We should all be feminists', published in 2014 (Elle, 2014 – reading log no. 39). This shows the influence of politics on fashion as a current issue of feminism (relating to issues such as the gender pay gap and getting more women involved in male dominated jobs, such as in the world of technology) has had a big enough impact on one of the world's biggest fashion houses that they designed a garment based upon it that ended up being a bestseller. As well as this, it has reignited the issue of feminism in the world once more, with the hashtag '#weshouldallbefeminists' getting over 22,000 posts on Instagram since the launch of the book and T-shirt (Instagram, 2017).

Research question one: What influences women in politics to dress the way they do?

This is the initial question which will be focused on because from here the other two research questions can develop. After extensive research, the hypothesis is that this is one of the initial ways that fashion influences politics. Clearly, there are many things that may influence a woman to dress in a certain way, and these will be explored below.

The first thing that influences women to dress the way they do is their own personal style as, fundamentally, what they wear is their decision. It is widely thought that a person's style reflects and affects their mood, their health, and overall confidence (Ferguson, 2017). Style involves the two factors of the symbolic meaning of the clothes you're wearing, and the physical experience of actually wearing them occurring at the same time. For example, a woman who works from home has the choice of putting on either comfortable clothes, such as a tracksuit, or a smart skirt suit which she would most likely have to wear if she were to work in an office. The comfortable clothes may be tempting, but might she be more empowered, strong, and productive in the smarter clothes? A study from Business Insider in 2014 showed that one's choice of clothing does not just affect confidence, but success too, and this is because 'clothing significantly influences how others perceive you, and how they respond to you' (Ferguson, 2017). From the primary research, respondent Anthea McIntyre (who is a

British Conservative Party member of the European Parliament for the West Midlands) said: 'If a politician doesn't appear to have taken any care with their appearance it looks as if they have no respect for their audience. I think people are more critical of women's dress than of men's' (See Appendix A). If we take this back to the example, a woman turning up to a business meeting with an important client would not be taken seriously at all if she turned up to an office in casual clothes while everyone else was in smart work attire. A client would be more likely to assume that the woman was less presentable than her colleagues and was wearing clothes inappropriate for the corporate surroundings and would therefore be less likely to take the work seriously. Considering all of this can be assumed from one outfit, it shows the importance of a person's style.

Similar to this, a personal style has usually developed from elements of childhood, upbringing and general beliefs. For example, Margaret Thatcher came from a humble background where her mother was a seamstress. Between the ages of fourteen and forty Thatcher and her sister regularly wrote letters to each other. Going through these letters, Thatcher's biographer, Charles Moore, found that she had written to her sister that she saw her wardrobe as 'an armour to do battle among the army of suit wearing men' (Jones, 2016 – reading log no. 1). This clearly demonstrates Thatcher's strength in wanting to be taken seriously by the then male dominated UK parliament, whom she subsequently became superior to. The dominant Zimbabwe newspaper 'Sunday News' said in 2015 that 'politicians should dress in an outfit that commands respect' (Matika, 2015 – reading log no. 30), and this is exactly what she did. It also showed the world that a female had the ability and stamina to be in a political position of power and become dominant over all of the men who doubted her competence. Without social media Thatcher was made world famous and so her style was portrayed in newspapers and magazines worldwide. Moving into more recent times, and the rise of social media, women's media profiles have an increasingly key role to play in the influence of their style. The best example of this is the first lady of the United States (FLOTUS) from 2008 to 2017, Michelle Obama. In 2009, Obama wore a white gown designed by Jason Wu to the inauguration ball. As Wu is a New York based designer it highlighted Obama's support for US designers as well as her patriotism. After 2009, Jason Wu was thrust into the spotlight in the fashion industry and became a more well-known label, now with shows at most major world fashion shows. His ready-to-wear collections are a huge success, with prices averaging around £2,000 per item of clothing (Vingan-Klein, 2016 – reading log source no. 2). A key British example of political patriotism is the Prime Minister Theresa May, a keen follower of fashion, famous for her leopard print kitten heels. She is regularly seen wearing pieces by British designer Amanda Wakeley, of whom May is a regular customer and keen supporter of the brand. To add to this, Nicola Sturgeon, the First Minister of Scotland, often chooses to wear designs by smaller Scottish brands like 'Totty Rocks' for public appearances (Bullock, 2016 – reading log no. 10). This demonstrates how clothing is a key way to establish a first impression as it immediately gives a positive impression of patriotism.

Often due to the high profile of women involved in global politics and international relations, partly as a result of social media, they get support from highly established brands which further helps the brands themselves to receive publicity. An example of this is Ralph Lauren who is an 'unabashed' Hillary Clinton supporter and therefore designed her now iconic red, white and blue trouser suits in 2016 during the presidential debates as well as the democratic nomination (The Telegraph, 2016 – reading log no. 3).

Females involved in politics who break down gender stereotypes are widely praised, because, as well as their political involvement, it shows how they use their large following to spread a positive message. The key thing is that unlike politics, which many people choose not to follow or do not understand, fashion and the female gender stereotypes that come with that are relatable to more people, which is why it is such a big deal when it is achieved. For example, Hillary Clinton's famous trouser suits – predominantly designed by Ralph Lauren (Telegraph, 2016) – show that successful women can wear smart, stylish trousers without appearing masculine while not trying to emulate the actions of a man, just trying to be politically heard. At the same time, French politician and MEP Rachida Dati (Harper's Bazaar, 2016 – reading log no. 5) once said that 'As soon as you dress in too feminine a fashion, you get criticised', so it is possible that Clinton chose to dress in a slightly more masculine way in order to maintain the focus on her political agenda and not on her choice of fashion – would this be the same for men? In previous eras, power dressing meant dressing like a man. For example, female Pharaoh Hatshepsut, 1507BC–1458BC, used to wear a fake beard to establish her authority (Harper's Bazaar, 2016). This is comparable to today, when women such as Angela Merkel wear beige suits, 'adopting the uniform of the patriarchy as a sartorial signifier of belonging' (Harper's Bazaar, 2016). Margaret Thatcher believed that clothes were fundamental to her success and saw her wardrobe as 'an armour to do battle among the army of suit wearing men'. These three different examples clearly show the depth of the issue as evidence dates back over 3,500 years. But why is this still an issue, and why has there been no solution to gender equality – especially in the workplace? Why has there not been a solution that means that women and men are considered equally competent, irrespective of what they wear?

When something becomes a staple in a person's wardrobe, there are multiple reasons for this, which is a conclusion I have drawn myself. Firstly, they are clearly comfortable and confident in these clothes, possibly due to the help of a stylist, secondly, it may be due to their own preferences (if they dress themselves), or, thirdly, because of past positive reactions from people, for example a positive article in the media. In the case of Thatcher, she carried a box bag around on so many occasions that the term 'handbagging' was coined by the media for the way she shut down her political opponents. It was added to the Oxford English dictionary and is defined as 'the treatment of a person ruthlessly or insensitively' (Oxford dictionary). An example of such treatment was to Michael Portillo, former cabinet minister, when Thatcher 'swivelled vigorously on her heels, jabbed her finger at Michael Portillo and said: 'Michael, have you ever won a war? I have!', (Stone-Lee, 2013 – reading log no. 41). This shows how such a staple, repeated choice of clothing can have a lasting effect on society and is still reported on years after her leadership and death.

A woman's political allegiance is another key factor which influences how she dresses. In the 16th century European courts different styles of clothing were worn to mark the person's political allegiance. Foreign styles of dress indicated more power as the wearer assumed a higher profile on the broader political stage of Europe, although at this time they were all men. With women, many used to continue wearing the attire of their home country after their marriage to a foreign man. For example, Anne of Cleeves continued with her Germanic style of dress after her marriage to Henry VIII (Cox Rearick, 2009 – reading log no. 17). This has decreased in the contemporary age although, as previously mentioned, dressing patriotically is common among women to show support for designers in their own country. Additionally, it is common when visiting foreign countries for women to wear something affiliated with that country as a mark of respect. For example, on a visit to Japan in August 2017, Theresa May wore a red dress with a white jacket, the same colours as the Japanese flag, indicating clear thought and respect.

Research question 2: Does the way a woman dresses affect how they come across to the public (and how has it changed?)

After a Brexit discussion meeting in March 2017 in Glasgow, Theresa May (Prime Minister) was photographed along with Nicola Sturgeon (First Minister of Scotland), both wearing skirt suits which showed their legs. This sparked a huge amount of debate among the media as to whether their choices of dress were acceptable. The purpose of the meeting had been forgotten and was barely commented on which is questionable considering how important Brexit is for the UK at the present time. The photo apparently qualified for one of the 'basic big three' that a photo should ideally have for media scrutiny. These include adversaries in close proximity, an ongoing style off, or revealing personal details. The media coined the term 'Legs it' as the photo was published (Malkin, 2017 – reading log no. 43). This media reaction is similar to when Theresa May wore leather trousers from luxury British clothing brand Amanda Wakeley, and the term 'Leathergate' was created by the media, a play on words of the 'Watergate' scandal in America in 1972. After the 'Legs it' photograph was published in British newspapers, May joked 'You will notice I am wearing trousers. As a woman in politics throughout my whole career I have found very often, what I wear has been an issue that has been looked at rather closely by people. I think that most people concentrate on what we do as politicians. But if people want to have a bit of fun about how we dress, then so be it.' The reaction of the public to the outfit was clearly anticipated, otherwise the media would not have published the article and would have written something that would get more readers. This demonstrates how the focus of the general public has changed as the attention of the articles was not focused on the detail of the meeting but on what the attendees wore. If social media was not so prominent in our current lives, would this still be the case? Probably not, as newspapers would print articles that were deemed necessary and newsworthy, and the choice of a woman's clothing used not to be. From the primary research it was found that politicians in the local area, not necessarily operating on a national level, had been told that in order to succeed as a female political candidate, trousers should not be worn and nor should black clothing, 'I have personally been told that to succeed as a female candidate I should not wear trousers, and not wear black suits/dress'. This further presents the point of whether or not this is socially acceptable guidance in the workplace, and why this guidance has not changed (see Appendix A – response from McKay).

In the 1970s and 1980s, there was a similar story about Margaret Thatcher, the then prime minister. Her iconic handbags gave her a symbol as a fighter and a warrior because she worked and debated with politicians every day who were mainly men, and they therefore made her stand out. There was a similar situation in 2016 in America, when fashion became more political when Hillary Clinton became the first woman ever nominated for US president by one of the two major parties. The trend began around the 2008 election, the time when she was competing for the Democratic nomination for president but lost out to Obama; 'a lot of female designers decided to stand next to Clinton,' (Weiner, 2017 – reading log no. 40). From Clinton's style transformation other women, such as Nancy Pelosi, the current minority leader of the House of Representatives, decided to do the same. Especially in America, the more frequent elections and the arguable 'celebrity style' of politicians means that there is more opportunity for the media to comment on their styles and make stories from them. As the use of social media has increased, it is arguable that the way a woman dresses and the way it affects how the woman comes across to the public has changed because there are an increasing number of platforms for people to publish their opinions, and a wider audience to read them; the millions of users of social and online media combined with the readers of traditional print media. From the primary research, Baroness Emma Pidding stated that 'it is much easier for a woman in politics to get noticed or to be remembered because of the clothes that she wears to establish your individual brand/style'. From this, it can be concluded that despite the negative connotations surrounding the use of social media as a platform to express views on women's fashion choices it helps to create conversation around a politically involved woman, helping her receive media attention which could result in more focus being put on her political career. This shows the dynamic nature of both the political and media worlds as the audience and readers of media increased within the time period of the contemporary age.

Why is what women in politics wear such a big issue? Why does it make headlines? Part of the reason is because in the time of Thatcher there weren't many women involved in politics in the UK and so the media were adapting and writing about what the public wanted to hear, and politics is always an appropriate topic to write about because it is ever changing. As soon as a woman came to such a position of power, (she became Prime Minister in 1979), there was an entirely new scope of topics to write about to do with her attitude and different clothing, not to mention her seemingly radical right-wing policies. Traditionally, politics and fashion were considered 'entirely separate domains' (Weiner, 2017 – reading log no. 40), but now, new designers are questioning the world between fashion and politics and using their designs to express their political views, whether this is through blunt slogans on T-shirts, or by not using fur or leather in their collections. This in itself is creating a more comprehensive interest in politics that has been lacking in Britain for so long. This sense of apathy is slowly diminishing, and more and more young people are starting to realise the importance of participating in politics and making their voices heard. At the 2017 general election on 9 June, the turnout among the youngest category of voters, 18–24 years old was 64% (Burn-Murdoch, 2017), the highest it has been since 1992 when turnout was 67%. Due to this demographic and the changing of the electorate, political parties may have to start aiming more of their manifestos towards the younger generation, putting a stop to the stereotype that politics is for the 'white, pale, male, and old' section of society. This shows the extent that fashion and politics are becoming more closely associated through the younger people that actively take an interest in both, (unintentionally) encouraging others to do the same. Millennials, especially, are more socially conscious and more liberal than their older counterparts were at the same age and so are bridging fashion and politics, using clothing to express their beliefs and to demonstrate their commitment to social causes, and if fashion is in 'some way increasing the general interest in politics, then that is no bad thing' (Lever, 2010 – reading log no. 28).

Research question 3: How far does the designer's influence or political stance come across in their collections?

Ahead of the 2016 inauguration ball for Donald Trump there was much debate over who would dress Melania Trump because of her obvious affiliation with her husband. Top designers such as Marc Jacobs and Tom Ford publicly refused to dress her, which caused speculation in the media as to who would be willing to take on this important job which has driven previous designers into the fashion spotlight. Karl Lagerfeld (creative director at Chanel) was briefly considered a choice, but this choice would break the first unwritten rule of designing the garment, which is the appointment of a non-American (Telegraph, 2015 – reading log no. 3) for such a significant point in American history. But considering Melania is Slovenian, was this really as big an issue compared to other future first ladies? As the final designer of the ballgown was decided to be Hervé Pierre, a French / American designer, it clearly was of lesser importance.

During New York fashion week in 2017 protest T-shirts were a common sight. These were predominantly designed in relation to Trump's harsh policies on immigration since becoming president, for example, his promise to build a wall between Mexico and America to prevent more Hispanic immigrants entering the country. Nepalese American designer Prabal Gurung created T-shirts with slogans such as 'revolution has no borders' and 'this is what a feminist looks like', which were inspired by a women's march he attended in New York in January of that year (Bryant, 2017 – reading log no. 8). Other designers did similar things, like the Dior 'we should all be feminists' T-shirt, and Christian Siriano's 'make American New York', and 'people are people' T-shirts. This shows the pace with which the fashion industry moves and how it easily reflects the 'sentiment of its consumers', while clearly demonstrating the designer's own political views within their works. It is also being said that 'fashion reflects the social climate of a given time period' as it is fast moving, and responsive to current affairs.

British designer Vivienne Westwood is famous for her outgoing political views, not only through her designs. For example, she has openly stated that she supported the independence of Scotland (Waters, 2017 – reading log no. 27), is a keen supporter of the Green party, and thought Thatcher was hypocritical. Through the large following that she has (the brand has over 1 million followers on Instagram), she is easily able to portray her thoughts to many people, encouraging them to think the same. One example of this is through her support of the Green party as she supports the movement of ethical fashion in her designs. She is one of Ethical Fashion Initiative's first partners, and from this she has designed and made collections such as the 'made with love' collection which was created using recycled canvas and used leather offcuts. Related ethical issues such as these (inequality, sweat shops) have been named as some of the top ten issues in the fashion business (Houston Chronicle, 2016 – reading log no. 31), as they can reflect badly on the wearer. As can be seen from this, Westwood is one the designers whose political stance comes across the most strongly in the fashion world as the designs and points she makes are often bold, for example in her AW15 menswear shows models were made to look bruised to symbolise eco warriors on a mission to save the environment. This is contrasted to other (seemingly less bold) decisions such as Stella McCartney's to use faux leather and fur in her collections. Nevertheless, actions such as this are still a step in the right direction to becoming increasingly eco-friendly, adapting into incorporating changing environmental views such as the rise of veganism and the distaste for leather within designs. This in itself helps to break down the stereotypes of the fashion industry as unadaptable, self-absorbed and excessive.

Discussion to research question 1: What influences women in politics to dress the way they do?

Can your choice of clothing really affect how you perform? According to the Washington Post, wearing clothes associated with certain qualities could help improve performance. Even if this was the case, would performance be the primary reason you would choose to wear a certain garment? The Kellogg School of Management completed a study to see if this theory was legitimate, calling it 'enclothed recognition', similar to the study of 'embodied recognition' that examined whether bodily sensations can affect how we think and feel. They also found that the symbolic meaning behind the clothes encourages performance too. Although this study focused only on the white coats worn by artists, there are some similarities that can be drawn from this in relation to a person's choice of clothing. If, when wearing the clothes you have put on, you associate them with power and confidence it is going to have a greater impact on your productivity and function than if you do not. From the research undertaken, respondent Emma Ideson said: 'Feeling good about appearance makes you present yourself strongly and adds confidence'. A similar thing was said by Diana Wallis MEP, who said that 'dressing smartly can also give you confidence about how you feel and how you project yourself' (See Appendix A). This could depend on the character of the person. If you do not associate certain clothes with certain emotions this theory is less likely to apply. Another note from the study was that this could wear off after time, and as people become more 'habituated' with their clothes, the effects of wearing them are decreasingly present. Despite this, it could be down to workplace culture. If a woman MP did not wear a smart suit when sitting in the House of Commons it would be unusual and she would be looked down upon and considered 'too casual'. The act of not wanting to stand out as unusual could be the simplest driving factor.

Although general beliefs are somewhat rooted into a person

throughout their whole life, as their careers change and develop, as well as their general lives, these beliefs are still likely to change. As a result of this the style and choice of clothing itself changes along with the beliefs. For example, if right from childhood you were taught that being smart and well-dressed was extremely important you are likely to carry this through to your adult working life. If circumstances changed (regarding your work life) and you began to work from home this may change because you are no longer travelling to a corporate building with people dressed in a similar way to you.

With the huge increase in the use of social media, there is a bigger platform for the clothes that someone wears to be commented on. Positions such as the first lady often receive comments from the media, for example, Michelle Obama's inauguration ball dress designed by Jason Wu caused uproar. Her choice of clothing was a vital step toward Wu becoming the world-famous designer that he now is, which is obviously a positive step. In the UK figures such as Theresa May often get poor comments from the media regarding their clothing choices, with key examples being the 'Leathergate' scandal (a play on the Watergate scandal of 1972) and her trademark leopard print kitten heels. Criticism from the media often includes how expensive the garments are. When May was seen carrying a leather handbag from Amanda Wakeley that cost £995 in 2016 (Telegraph 2017 – reading log no. 4), MP Nicky Morgan attacked May saying that she would never spend this much on an accessory herself. Morgan was then hit by a backlash with people calling her rude for criticising how another person spent their money, which many agreed with. Why should someone have to justify to millions of people why and how they have spent their money? In 2015, after the Women of the World event, even before she was Prime Minister, Theresa May, then Home Secretary, said about press stories about her clothes: 'I am a woman and I like clothes. I like shoes and I like clothes. I think one of the challenges for women in politics and in business and working life is actually to be ourselves. You know what, you can be clever and like clothes. You can have a career and like clothes.' After researching and thinking about this further it is clear this quote shared the problems that women in the working world face, thinking that fashion and politics or business do not go together, and that when a woman is interested in fashion she is thought of as less intelligent or less educated than people in traditional white collar jobs, and somehow this makes the person less intelligent or less focused on their working life. In a quote, writer and feminist Chimamanda Ngozi Adichie said this about the Western culture: 'Women who wanted to be taken seriously were supposed to substantiate their seriousness with a studied indifference to appearance', which complements the comments made by Theresa May.

Discussion to research question 2: Does the way a woman dresses affect how they come across to the public (and how has it changed)?

After a Daily Mail article was published in 2017 regarding the Brexit meeting between May and Sturgeon with the title: 'Never Mind Brexit, who won Legs-it!' Sarah Vine, the journalist who wrote the article, referred to Sturgeon's legs as 'altogether more flirty, tantalisingly crossed … a direct attempt at seduction' (Vine, 2017). Unsurprisingly, this received a huge backlash from many important political figureheads, both male and female, with Jeremy Corbyn (in political opposition) commenting, 'this sexism must be consigned to history' (Guardian, 2017 – reading log no. 40). Sexism on a national scale like this was thought to be a thing of the past in Britain, and, predominantly through social media, Vine was publicly shamed for writing such a vindictive piece for the Daily Mail. Social media platforms such as Twitter allowed users to come together and show their distaste for the backward and disrespectful piece of writing that was published, showing how for the majority of the population times have moved on and to talk about a female for the way she dresses is nothing but unacceptable. French politician Rachida Dati said in 2013 that 'As soon as you dress in too feminine a fashion, you get criticised', and this is exactly the case, which poses the question of what is too feminine. It should be argued that the idea that a woman must dress in a more masculine way in order to be taken seriously in the working world is absurd; why should dressing in a way deemed 'too feminine' when you're a woman mean you should receive criticism?

Ironically, in the time of Thatcher (Prime Minister 1979–1990), her choice of dress was a way for her to stand out and compete against the predominantly male parliament. Despite some comments, she was standing from a position of strength because her strategies of dressing well to appear confident and dominant worked, and she was stereotyped as a strong leader with undeniable power. In 2017, although there are many more women in parliament, social media as well as print media have allowed political figureheads to be seen as weaker and more vulnerable to the press because more people use their right of free speech to express their opinion through social media allowing politicians to be publicly mocked. This was only the case in print media for Thatcher.

From the research conducted (see Appendix A), it was found first-hand how women in today's society are still explicitly told what and what not to wear in order to be successful. In this particular case Christine McKay was told that wearing trousers or black clothes would not bring her the success in her political career as a local conservative MP for the constituency of Hull West that she desired. These suggestions were made worse by the fact that a man wearing a three-piece suit had given her the recommendations, which somewhat reinforces the idea of sexism in the political workplace as it is as well-known fact that the UK political world is heavily male dominated, and the idea of men telling women what to wear, as an ultimatum for success, is ludicrous. Similarly, Baroness Emma Pidding stated that 'In order to achieve any level of influence of power it sometimes feels that one needs to conform, and that individuality, even in clothing, is not to be encouraged' (see Appendix A), agreeing with the view that in order for success to be more likely conformation to society's norms is vital. On the other hand, if this advice is genuinely meant in a positive way with the guarantee of being taken more seriously as a woman if you were to dress as advised, does that make it acceptable? It can be seen as a temporary solution to a wider, deeper rooted problem in political society. It can be argued that, despite the anti-feminist connotations of what was said, if success was made more likely as a result the advice would be taken on board. However, the advice given to McKay was not relevant to the opinions of the general public, but instead the aim was to impress a group of 'retired party members' who select the MP at a local level. This shows that how she dressed had a direct effect on her success. As a result, the smaller scale of the issue in this case did not so much affect how McKay came across to the public as the event was more local. Despite this, McKay did say that she is always careful to dress in an 'understated' way, that involves covering her legs in order for attention to remain focused on the activity going on. This approach was not followed by Theresa May and Nicola Sturgeon in 2017, which sparked the 'Legs it' media response, and as a result there was a significant amount of attention to the fact that the two women were both bare legged. But, as the issue of Brexit is arguably of more national importance than local political issues, there was inevitably considerable coverage of what was actually said in the meeting, and thus this affected how they came across to the public more dramatically. Respondent Wendy Morton stated that 'the media can be very critical of how public figures dress…it is always about getting the balance right between what is appropriate for the job and what I want to wear as an individual… Parliament is often seen as a very grey place, that is changing – albeit slowly'. Comparably, Baroness Emma Pidding said that 'it is hard to ignore this media scrutiny, so this must have an influence on how our female politicians dress' (see Appendix A). Interestingly, this recognition of brutal media scrutiny was common across most of the research, showing how it definitely has an effect on most female politicians because if they are influential enough, it could make headlines on a local and national level.

Discussion to research question 3: How far does the designer's influence or political stance come across in the collections?

There is much debate over whether the unwritten rules of the inauguration ball dress should exist, one of which is that an American designer should produce it. This is because it is seen as patriotic and respectful to the country the first lady is about to become a representative of. This patriotism occurs worldwide, especially when visiting other countries, for example, in August 2017, Theresa May wore white and red, which are the colours of the Japanese flag, on a trip to Tokyo as a sign of respect to the country being visited. On one hand, being faithful to American brands helps bring fame and business to native brands and therefore an increased chance of worldwide success while helping the domestic economy by keeping money within the US. However, in the modern day or the contemporary age buying from foreign countries is not an issue at any other time or for any other person. The convention of American designers dressing the future first lady is prominent and invoking a negative media reaction for not 'staying native' is not ideal when so new in the role of first lady.

Although protest T-shirts have been around for years, 2017 was the first time that they dominated the runways at fashion weeks. This shows the extent of the political turmoil the US has been in since the inauguration of Trump in November 2016. The shirts changed the way that fashion had been stereotyped as it allowed people to see how reactive fashion can be to current affairs and that it did not simply repeat the same thing show after show. This has increased with the rise in more controversial politics, for example with Trump's strong views on immigration and his plans to build a wall on the American border with Mexico. As a result, the runways and other areas in which designs are shown have become alternative platforms to voice an opinion. Again, as the use of cable television and social media has increased there has been more coverage of fashion weeks and therefore more spreading of opinions from the public.

Designers such as Westwood are an example of how social media can be used to portray an opinion and a positive message about the ethics of high fashion. It is well known for the fashion industry to be a harsh one, and styles such as Westwood's are welcomed by the half (23.1 million) of Britain's consumers who think ethical production of the clothes they buy is important (TNS Worldpanel Fashion, 2008). In this way, she is one of the high fashion brand names that associate fashion and politics closely regarding ethical and environmental issues within fashion. This allows their consumers to associate the two, while shining a spotlight on ethical issues that are prevalent in today's fashion world, especially highlighting the increasing environmental damage that the textile industry causes, for example through the use of leather. As well as showcasing her opinions and work to the public, Westwood emphasises to designers what they too could be doing to make a difference in their industry, and to focus on what the industry needs to move away from, because the popularity of the industry can so easily be used to unintentionally send out negative messages (for example of not being environmentally conscious) to its consumers.

EPQ CONCLUSION

From the extensive research, it can be concluded that there is indeed a link between fashion and politics. This project has been split into the above three questions to try to distinguish an answer to 'How have fashion and politics influenced each other, through women, in the contemporary age?' This has led to the conclusion that how a woman wants to present herself to the public is one of the driving factors and, especially regarding women with an interest in fashion, this choice helps to launch established and new designers, both further into the world of fashion and into the world of politics, as more of a connection is made between the designer and the area of politics they have established themselves in. In most of the cases in this research, this has been the result of one of two things. Firstly, new designers are chosen by political figures, especially in the case of first ladies choosing the designer of their inauguration ball dress. Secondly, the way that designers choose to convey their political ideas in their designs helps to further blur the line between the once separated topics of fashion and politics. The primary data collected from the questionnaire shows that although fashion may not necessarily be the main priority for women involved in politics it certainly is a contributing factor to how they present themselves. In addition, the media plays a substantial role in how women are presented to the public, and, in some ways, this has placed a focus on the negative relationship between fashion and politics through the constant criticism of women with a high profile in politics.

Over time women's role in fashion has changed as how women dress has received increased coverage in the media. To some extent women are used as a medium to connect the two worlds of politics and fashion together in what was once a male dominated environment.

As there has been an increase in controversial politics, especially since the inauguration of Trump as president, there has been a rise in the amount of politics seen in fashion, especially on the runways. This is because as fashion gets an increasing amount of media coverage there is a wider audience for a designer to express their political views. These views are likely to be similar to many others, as fashion on the runways takes much of its inspiration from current affairs and people, because ultimately it is people that model, buy and wear these clothes, hugely contributing to the success of fashion houses and businesses.

APPENDIX A:
QUESTIONNAIRE AND RESPONSES RECEIVED

The four questions formulated for the short questionnaire were:

1. **How do you think the way you, and indeed other female politicians, dress affects the way you come across to the public?**
2. **Does the way you dress affect how you make decisions (politically)? If so, how and why?**
3. **What does the term 'power dressing' mean to you?**
4. **Do you believe that the interest of the media in women's fashion influences the way females involved in politics dress, or portray themselves?**

The questionnaire was sent to:

-   Emma Ideson (involved in local politics in Yorkshire)
-   Anthea McIntyre (British Conservative Party member of the European Parliament for the West Midlands)

- Wendy Morton (Conservative MP for the constituency of Aldridge-Brownhills in the West Midlands, and currently serving as assistant government whip)
- Christine McKay (prospective Conservative Party candidate for West Hull and Hessle in Yorkshire, and the chair of the Hessle Conservative branch)
- Diana Wallis MEP (former member of the European Parliament for Yorkshire and the Humber for the Liberal Democrats, and candidate for the Yorkshire First party)
- Baroness Emma Pidding (British Conservative parliamentarian and currently serving as a life peer in the House of Lords).

RESPONSE FROM EMMA IDESON:

1. How do you think the way you, and indeed other female politicians, dress affects the way you come across to the public?

Appearance is very important to me. As a business woman I like to wear smart trouser suits and heels. Feeling good about appearance makes you present yourself strongly and adds confidence. There is nothing worse than dealing with scruffy/ill-dressed women. Taking pride in your appearance gives a strong presentation. I prefer to wear black/navy and neutral colours – however, I do admire women who wear stronger coloured suits. Before Corbyn got his makeover (pre GE) he was the epitome of scruffy and his dress was highly inappropriate.

2. Does the way you dress affect how you make decisions (politically)? If so, how and why?

I am not sure it affects making decisions – I feel dress is what gives a good impression (or bad) – but I don't think it changes decisions made.

3. What does the term 'power dressing' mean to you?

Power dressing normally makes me think of the 80s and shoulder pads – I think it's a softer version in this day and age. But power dressing is wearing smart suits and shoes, still keeping feminine – but looking the part. We all remember

Margaret Thatcher's blouse neck lines – she was famous for them – and I liked it when Samantha Cameron repeated those drape necklines on a couple of occasions.

4. Do you believe that the interest of the media in women's fashion influences the way females involved in politics dress, or portray themselves?
Yes I believe it does influence. A female politician wants to do her job – not be singled out for inappropriate dress

RESPONSE FROM ANTHEA MCINTYRE:

1. How do you think the way you, and indeed other female politicians, dress affects the way you come across to the public?

I think the way people dress has a considerable effect on the way they come across to the public and this is true of both male and female politicians. If a politician doesn't appear to have taken any care with their appearance it looks as if they have no respect for their audience. I think people are more critical of women's dress than of mens. People will comment about a woman that 'her skirt is too short' or 'that colour doesn't suit her', which they would not say about a man, but they will comment that he or she 'looks untidy/scruffy'. The way a politician dresses will be interpreted by those around them, so it is important to put out the message that you want people to receive.

2, Does the way you dress affect how you make decisions (politically)? If so, how and why?

No, I don't think so.

3. What does the term 'power dressing' mean to you?

Dressing to try to impress people that you are a powerful person.

4, Do you believe that the interest of the media in women's fashion influences the way females involved in

politics dress, or portray themselves?

Yes, I think it does. This can sometimes cause people to dress in the opposite way to the latest fashion to make a statement that they 'do not follow fashion' or that 'they are their own person'. As a woman it isn't always easy to be taken seriously so that, too, influences what politicians wear. If someone is campaigning for something, then minimising anything that would be a negative is worth doing. Dressing so as to not upset anyone, to be taken seriously etc. is a good policy!

RESPONSE FROM WENDY MORTON:

1. How do you think the way you, and indeed other female politicians, dress affects the way you come across to the public?

I take the view that I am the elected representative of my constituency, and my constituents would expect me to reflect that in my behaviour and appearance.

Furthermore, I believe it's important to dress in a manner that is appropriate for the job that you do. Politics and Parliament is no different in that regard. For example I will always dress smartly when I am in Parliament, but in contrast when I am in the constituency doing community based visits or activities I am more likely to dress in a more casual manner, and yes that may sometimes mean jeans. It depends entirely on what I am doing, but I do want to be 'me'.

As a female in Parliament though there are certain things to be aware of such as the length of your skirt and the neckline of your dress as debates in the Chamber and Westminster Hall are recorded and can be televised, as are committee proceedings.

2. Does the way you dress affect how you make decisions (politically)? If so how and why?

I think it's fair to say that the way I dress does not in any way affect how I make decisions.

3. What does the term 'power dressing' mean to you?

The term Power Dressing somehow conjures up images from the 1980s - Dallas and Dynasty - big shoulder pads, high heels, very sharp tailoring and images from the fashion and TV of that era.

In today's world both men and women can certainly dress to get noticed be that in Parliament or elsewhere but I don't think the term power dressing is quite what it was.

4. Do you believe that the influence of the media in women's fashion influences the way females involved in politics dress, or portray themselves?

The media can be very critical of how public figures dress, especially female MPs, as we have seen on several occasions. Fashion and style is about personality and for me, as someone working in politics, it is always about getting the balance right between what is appropriate for the job and what I want to wear as an individual. For example, I like colours and there are certain colours I particularly like and so I will wear them. Parliament is often seen as a very grey, male-dominated place. That is changing - albeit slowly - look at the colour on the green benches today!

RESPONSE FROM CHRISTINE MCKAY:

1. How do you think the way you, and indeed other female politicians, dress affects the way you come across to the public?

I feel that it is very unusual for a female politician to attract positive commentary about the way we look and dress, but common to attract negativity. Even the PM, who is in the minority of those who have positive press about her fashion choices, has reporters arguing over the appropriateness of cleavage or a split skirt.

I have personally been told that to succeed as a female candidate I should not wear trousers, and not wear black suits/dress – this by a male in a three-piece pinstripe and whilst attending a 'candidates training event' – albeit 6 years ago. I am not sure that the 'general public' care about this, and advice was perhaps aimed at impressing an audience of retired party members who select the MP locally.

At official events when representing the Party I am generally careful to dress in a neutral understated way, always minimally made up and never bare legged for example. This takes away potential discussion from how I might be dressed and allows the focus to be on the activity, speech etc. - where I want the attention to be.

So, the way I dress affects the way I come across to the public in that it doesn't detract or distract, is not the focus, and never lowers me in their estimation. Or at least that is the hope.

2. Does the way you dress affect how you make decisions (politically)? If so, how and why?

No. The decision always comes first.

3. What does the term 'power dressing' mean to you?

I feel that power dressing has evolved from 'dressing like a man,' or being suited and booted (Merkel e.g.). but I am not sure those within the Party necessarily agree. In order to achieve any level of influence or power it sometimes feels that one needs to conform, and that individuality, even in clothing, is not to be encouraged.

My personal opinion is that power has no uniform, and that quality clothing worn with confidence by a woman in a position of power should be a matter of her taste. The issue is when a woman is not in a position or power, but has ambition to get there, and particularly in a traditional male dominated hierarchical organisation such as a political Party. Individuality is not part of the culture, and I sometimes feel that diverse and confident women (generally, not just with clothing) are viewed with suspicion or as 'quirky'.

4. Do you believe that the interest of the media in women's fashion influences the way females involved in politics dress, or portray themselves?

Yes, for those who are interested in fashion. The rest of us learn from the 'mistakes' of other females, not necessarily dress mistakes but based on reports in the press about dress and appearance choices.

The PM makes clever choices in order perhaps to positive influence her audience, e.g. Wearing red and black for her recent visit to Japan, which made the news. I expect she will also not wear her expensive leather trousers again after being portrayed as being out of touch for doing so. It felt worse to me that it was another Conservative woman who made the comments and was a backward step for female politicians who want to be fashionable.

I feel the media interest in fashion forces women in politics to think twice about what we wear, when a man would certainly be less likely to be concerned about his choice of suit making the headlines.

My opinion based on the contrasting views re Corbyn vs Eagle for the Labour leadership:

A man might wear an unironed shirt, not dry clean his jacket if he wears one at all, or forget to comb his hair, and he might be portrayed as 'in touch with real people', ethical, a boffin/academic, eccentric (in a good way) etc.

A woman in a crumpled suit with bad hair and no make-up might be portrayed as 'losing it' and would not be considered to have the gravitas or authenticity afforded to the male.

RESPONSE FROM DIANA WALLIS MEP

1. How do you think the way you, and indeed other female politicians dress affects the way you come across to the public?

I think the way we dress can affect very much the way we come across in public. Clothes are an expression of our personality but those who view us also have their own preferences and expectations of how they think a female politician should dress. When I started my political career in the late 1980s I was a successful lawyer in London, so naturally I wanted to project that professional image especially when I was mainly competing against male colleagues to be selected for a seat. In any event I always felt that dressing smartly can also give you confidence about how you feel and how you project yourself. That said I don't think you need to be 'a female in a male suit' to succeed. I have always tended towards the more professional type clothes but then have also used bright coloured jackets, scarves etc. to be more feminine. I also think over the years things have become rather more relaxed anyway which is great.

2. Does the way you dress affect how you make decisions (politically)? If so, how and why?

Can't really see a relationship here at all if I am honest. There is a relationship in my view between dress, how you feel about yourself and general confidence, but I do not think this extends to 'decision-making' It is more obvious in how you perform in public situations particularly say delivering a key speech etc. which may influence other people but not during your own intellectual decision-making process.

3. What does the term 'power dressing' mean to you?

A term used several decades ago to denote women and men wearing normally smart business suits. Associated with the era of big shoulder pads etc. The opposite of Ken Clarke and his 'hush puppy' suede shoes!

RESPONSE FROM BARONESS EMMA PIDDING:

I answer these questions as a Member of the House of Lords. I believe that my responses also relate to Members of Parliament in the House of Commons. Of course, there are other guises of 'politicians' such as those involved in local government.

1. How do you think the way you, and indeed other female politicians dress affects the way you come across to the public?

A man in politics has a 'standard uniform'. Suit, shirt and tie (although the latter has seen recent controversy with the House of Commons Speaker announcing that a tie is not necessary for appearance of Members of Parliament in the Chamber!) see link:

http://www.bbc.co.uk/news/uk-politics-40446102

In the work place as well as in politics, the 'standard uniform' for a woman has never been as easily defined or straight forward.

I do not believe that the public are overly critical of how their politicians are dressed as long as they are 'appropriately dressed'. What is appropriate however, is another question!

The media scrutiny of women in politics (as well as women generally in the public eye) is excessive.

(I also believe that when a corporate uniform is required such as in some instances working for a Bank, Retail store, or even in the Armed Forces, it is a good leveller. The same could be said of school uniform.)

2. Does the way you dress affect how you make decisions (politically)? If so, how and why?

No. The way I dress does not affect how I make decisions.

3. What does the term 'power dressing' mean to you?

To me, the term 'power dressing' means being dressed to give yourself the utmost confidence when attending an important meeting, delivering a speech, etc. This confidence comes from feeling comfortable in what you are wearing, as well as feeling that you are looking your best.

I do not believe that 'power dressing' should be that different from your usual form of attire. However, it might well be a favourite suit, or jacket that is not worn every day but is kept for those important occasions. In some instances the use of colour can add 'power', in enabling you to stand out from a crowd.

4. Do you believe that the interest of the media in women's fashion influences the way females involved in politics dress, or portray themselves?

I do feel that the attention of the media on how our female politicians dress is disproportionate.

See link from Mail on Line below:
http://www.dailymail.co.uk/femail/article-

The hardcopy version of the paper was equally focussed on the detail of female cabinet member's attire!

It is hard to ignore this media scrutiny, so yes, this must have an influence on how our female politicians dress.

On the positive side, it is much easier for a woman in politics to get noticed or to be remembered because of the clothes / fashions that she wears. To establish your individual 'brand / style' i.e. :

Theresa May – shoes
Hillary Clinton – Pant Suits
Margaret Thatcher – Deep Blue Tailored Suits

Printed in Great Britain
by Amazon